KT-520-813

«When I first moved to Auteuil, the rue Raynouard still looke[d]
There are still oil lamps in the rue Berton, but no doubt the[y]

Guillaume Apollinaire, *Le Flâneur des deux rive[s]*

Historical background

The Maison de Balzac is one of the last vestiges of the village of Passy, which became annexed to the capital in 1860. Its origin goes back to the late XVIIIth century. At that time, the main building used to stand where the railings are now, but this was demolished when the rue Raynouard was widened in 1937. The garden was reached by an inside staircase, and in the garden was another house, equally erected on the side of the hill, the second floor of which overlooked, as it still does today, the rue Berton. Gérard de Nerval visited Balzac here, and gives the following description :

«One called at a little door nestling in a street flanking the heights of Passy, with a view extending as far as the Grenelle plain, île aux Cygnes and Champ-de-Mars.

There was no house to be seen, just a wall, a green door and a bell.

The concierge opened the door, and one suddenly found oneself coming down from the sky on to the first floor landing.

On the second floor, one came across the concierge's lodge, and was told that there were still two more floors below. At least this inverted house had no mezzanine.

The bottom floor opened out into a courtyard. Two terracotta busts down the far end indicated the novelist's abode. When the door opened, the most delicious smell greeted the attentive nostrils of the man of taste, — just like the smell of green apples referred to in Solomon.

This was the pantry, and on the meticulously laid-out shelves was every conceivable variety of Saint-Germain pear one could imagine.» (*La Presse*, 28th October 1850).

much as it had done in Balzac's time. It has changed a lot since.
vill also disappear in time.»

Signed by the author. Acquired in 1987, inv. 98

Hounded by both creditors and bailiffs, who were threatening to seize his furniture and put a court order on his property in Sèvres, Les Jardies, Balzac found a convenient refuge in the rue Basse (now rue Raynouard) in Passy. By going along the rue du Roc (now rue Berton), past the hôtel de Lamballe (which today houses the Turkish embassy), he could easily reach the capital by following the route de Versailles (now avenue de New-York) as far as the Bonshommes crossroads (now rue Beethoven), where the gate of Passy was situated. There he could board a ferry right into the centre of Paris. The position of his new home must also have appealed, with its south-facing study overlooking the garden, where he was allowed a brief respite, picking lilac and the first violets of the season for Madame Hanska, «which have come to this sunlit corner of Paris amidst the fumes of carbon dioxide, where books and flowers grow like mushrooms.» But the peace and quiet was only superficial. In 1844, he complained about the noise from children on the floor below. According to the land register, there were still fifteen tenants living in the house in 1862.

Between October 1840 and April 1847, Balzac was therefore living in a modest apartment on the second floor. The owner of the house was a rich butcher from Passy, Etienne-Désiré Grandemain. Balzac had adopted the pseudonym of Monsieur de Breugnol, inspired by his housekeeper whose name was Louise Breugniot, but who appears in the novels as Mme.de Breugnol or Brugnol. He had five rooms : the dining-room was opposite the front door, and the bedroom, sitting-room and study led off to the right ; on the left, behind the kitchen (now the ticket office) was the guest room. The «Passy cabin», as Balzac called it, was the scene of feverish creative activity; he corrected the whole of *The Human Comedy* here and also wrote some of his greatest works : *A Dark Affair*, *La Rabouilleuse*, *Ursule Mirouët*, *Splendours and Miseries of Courtisans*, *Cousin Bette*, *Cousin Pons*...

Exterior view
of Balzac's
house
photograph

Rue Berton
by Eugène Atget
photograph

The house was saved from ruin in 1910 and turned into a private museum. The Ville de Paris took it over in 1949. Today it includes Balzac's garden apartment, but also the rooms and outhouses originally occupied by the other tenants, and spans three levels between the rue Raynouard and the rue Berton.

The visitor may conjure up the old Passy with nostalgia, recalling the words of Béranger :

«Paris, farewell, I am leaving your city gates behind
In tranquil Passy peace and quiet I find»,

but he will soon realise that this unexpected oasis of calm is not merely the former house of the writer of *The Human Comedy*. The Maison de Balzac is also a museum, library and research centre, with a constantly increasing number of exhibitions and publications to its credit and a collection of paintings, prints, objects, books and signed documents which grows more prolific by the year.

This guide cannot therefore provide a step by step account of permanently located objects. Change and rotation of books, manuscripts and drawings is of the essence, not only to allow for exhibitions and recent acquisitions, but also to mitigate conservation problems, which are particularly acute when paper is involved.

The guide is therefore divided into themes rather than rooms. It hopes to provide information and references for the visitor. And above all to encourage him to return.

More information on the history and exterior and interior architecture of the house is available in *De la maison au musée*, dossier n°2 of the Maison de Balzac, published by Paris-Musées in 1987.

«...Balzac, in his prime, displayed signs of rude health quite out of keeping with the romantic greenish pallor of his peers. The blood running through his thoroughbred Tourangeot veins whipped his cheeks with a vigorous purple glow and warmly suffused his broad, sinuous lips, which were always ready to break into laughter ; a slight moustache and a beauty spot accentuated their outline without disguising it; his square nose, with its flaring nostrils, was divided into two lobes and was quite original and unique [...]. His forehead was wide, handsome and noble, white in contrast to his other features, marked only by a perpendicular furrow at the base of the nose ; swollen with the memory of places, it protruded noticeably above the eyebrows ; his mass of long, thick, dark hair was swept back like a lion's mane. As for his eyes, they were exceptional. There was quite incredible life, light and magnetism in them. Despite his sleepless nights, the sclera was pure and limpid, with a bluish tinge, like that of a child or a virgin, with two black diamonds inset, which shone from time to time with a rich golden glow : these were eyes to make an eagle flinch, which could pierce through walls and souls and kill a wild beast at a glance, they were the eyes of a sovereign, a prophet, a conqueror.»

Théophile Gautier, *L'Artiste*, 1858

Portrait of Balzac
by Bisson
1842
daguerreotype
inv. 93

«Yesterday I said to Gérard as a joke that I was not a fine enough fish to be cooked in oil.»

Letters to Madame Hanska, late March 1833.

The very first portrait of Balzac, which can now be found in the Tours museum, was made by Louis Boulanger in 1836. Until that date, there had been few drawings of him and only one lithograph, which was reproduced in several magazines, taken from one of the two carved caricatures by Dantan Jeune, which were on show at Susse's in the impasse des Panoramas in 1835 and are located today at the entrance to the museum.

«I will enclose Dantan's two plaster caricatures in my dispatch of 17th April. He has portrayed all the personalities of the day. In my case, he mainly pokes fun at my famous turquoise-studded cane with the carved gold head, which has immeasurably more success in France than all my literary works put together. On the personal level, his target is my weight ; I look like Louis XVIII.» (*Letters to Madame Hanska*, 30th March 1835).

A lithograph by Benjamin Roubaud appeared in the 12th October 1838 edition of *Le Charivari* showing once again a fat, beaming Balzac, but this time dressed in a monk's habit.

Dantan and Roubaud paved the way for a considerable number of so-called «serious» portraits as well as caricatures, which on the whole tended to concentrate on Balzac's external attributes, his stoutness, sartorial eccentricities and frank, jovial expression. These are now preserved in the print room and are displayed in rotation.

The collections also include two sculptures created during Balzac's lifetime (see study). The first is by an Italian artist, Alessandro Putinatti, whom Balzac met in 1837 while staying in Milan. «This statue was motivated purely by affection, which permeates the whole work (...) ; he didn't want anything for it. I had the greatest difficulty simply paying the costs and marble.» (*Letters to Madame Hanska*, 10th April 1837).

Caricature of
Balzac
by Dantan Jeune
1835
plaster
inv. 972

The second was the work of David d'Angers. Their correspondence provides a valuable account of the phases of the creative process : «I have been told (...) that your work of art has increased still further in size since you transposed it from clay to marble» (16th May 1844). «Your bust is quite finished now (...). I sincerely hope that your friends do not find the work unworthy of the great historian of the human heart» (12th January 1845). The portrait was not accepted for the Salon because its dedication was against the rules : «To his friend de Balzac. P.J. David d'Angers. 1844». Balzac, for his part, dedicated *The Curé de Tours* «to David, sculptor» and sent him *A Superior Woman* (*The Civil Service*) with a note which read «To his friend David d'Angers. De Balzac. Sculptors are not the only ones to graft.»

In the study, next to the original marble, which was cast in bronze and placed on the writer's grave in Père-Lachaise cemetery, there is a bronze medallion, which David executed in 1843, together with a the rough lead pencil sketch for another medallion : «David has given my sister the profile he drew for my medal, it is a work of art.» (*Letters to* Madame Hanska, 1st February 1843).

But of all these portraits the most moving and most precious is undoubtedly the original daguerreotype from the collections of Balzac's housekeeper, Louise Breugniot, which is displayed here in enlarged photographic form to preserve the original. It was taken by Bisson in May 1842, when Balzac was living in this house, and it enchanted the writer : «[...] I am mesmerised by the perfection of the lighting effects.[...] It is so stunningly true to life and so precise !" (*Letters to Madame Hanska*, 2nd May 1842).»

This picture set off another series of portraits, including serious drawings (Bertall) and cartoons. After Balzac's death, artists like Nadar and Rodin were to draw much of their inspiration from this iconographical treasure-trove.

Balzac was born in Tours on 20th May 1799. The house in which he was born, at 25, rue de l'Armée-d'Italie, now known as the rue Nationale, was bombed in 1940. In June 1807, he went to school at the Oratoriens de Vendôme. His memories and the intellectual experiences of this period are recounted in *Louis Lambert*.

Balzac actually left the Touraine area at the age of fifteen, but he often returned there to seek solace and inspiration, staying at the château de Saché as the guest of a family friend, Monsieur de Margonne. The château de Vonne, situated near Saché, was the model for Clochegourde manor in *The Lily of the Valley* ; la Grenardière, in St-Cyr-sur-Loire, where he stayed with Madame de Berny, lent its name to one of the *Scenes of private life*, in which Balzac describes the landscape he saw from the terraces of the house : «From there you overlook three Touraine valleys and view the cathedral suspended in the air like a filigree ornament.»

1, rue Cassini
by Regnier
inv. 313

The Balzac family moved to Paris in 1814. They set up home in the Marais area, at 40 (now 122), rue du Temple, although Balzac subsequently lived in a series of other houses in Paris. The «New Complete Road Map of Paris», which is displayed in the museum, traces Balzac's itinerary from his garret in the rue Lesdiguières, described in *The Magic Skin* and *Facino Cane*, to his final abode in the rue Fortunée, now renamed rue Balzac. Letters naturally exist emanating from these various addresses, but the Maison de Balzac also owns a collection of photographs and prints relating to Balzac's homes, including 17, rue des Marais-Saint-Germain (now rue Visconti), where Balzac set up his printing works, and an engraving of 1, rue Cassini, commissioned from Regnier for Madame Hanska. The writer at work is represented by a goat tied to a stake.

Balzac also acquired a property outside Paris in 1837, the Jardies in Sèvres : «I am busy with the workmen, putting the finishing touches to the house, which is straight out of opéra-comique; I intend to cut myself off from the world to work, and the people I like will come and visit me,» he wrote to Madame de Castries in August 1838. The planned and completed building work precipitated the seizure of the property, which was sold on 15th July 1841. Balzac was already forced into hiding in October 1840, however, and found refuge in Passy.

Balzac's father, Bernard-François, was born in the Tarn region in 1746 of peasant stock, the eldest of eleven children. He left home at the age of twenty-two to seek his fortune in Paris and in 1776 was made clerk of the master of the requests in the King's Council. Contrary to his son's later version, the Revolution did not put an end to Bernard-François' career : he occupied a number of posts in the Paris civil service and in 1795 was made director of rations and fodder for the 22nd military division in Tours. He gradually worked his way up the municipal ladder, becoming administrator of the general hospice and deputy mayor. An amusing anecdote sums up his social success : for his daughter Laurence's wedding, he had two different sets of invitation printed, one in the name of Balzac, for close friends, and another destined for mere acquaintances, signed de Balzac, the name his son adopted some years later.

In 1814, Bernard-François returned to Paris with his family and cunningly succeeded in upholding his rights under the Restoration. He died on 19th June 1829, the very year Balzac published *The Chouans*, the first novel written under his own name.

His letters reveal the insatiable curiosity and vivacity of this Gascon countryman, who passed on to his son his theories on vital fluid and longevity. He was a freemason and disciple of the encyclopaedists, a passionate advocate of liberty but also of moral and social values, which led him to publish four social pamphlets, now preserved in the Maison de Balzac.

His son was destined for a legal career, and was consequently articled to a solicitor, Maître Guillonnet-Merville, from November 1816 to March 1818. It was here that Balzac discovered the world of harsh social realities and the power of money. He was later to dedicate *Episode under the Terror* to his former employer, who shares some of Derville's character traits in *The Human Comedy*.

Portrait
of Bernard-François
Balzac
Anon.
circa 1795-1814
oil on canvas
inv. 95

Portrait of
Maître
Guillonnet-Merville
by J.B. Carbillet
1837
oil on canvas
inv. 543

«Do you know, my dear fellow, resumed Derville after a pause, "that there exist in our society three men, the priest, the doctor and the man of law, who cannot look up to the world ? They wear black robes, perhaps because they wear mourning for all the virtues, all the illusions. The most unfortunate of them is the solicitor. When a man comes in search of the priest, he comes to him urged on by repentance, by remorse, by those beliefs which render him interesting, which elevate him, and which bring some consolation to the soul of the mediator, whose task is not devoid of a sort of enjoyment ; he purifies, he repairs and reconciles. But we solicitors see the same evil sentiments repeating themselves, nothing corrects them, our offices are sewers that cannot be cleansed. How many things I have learned in the course of my profession ! I have seen a father die in a garret, without a sou or a stitch, abandoned by two daughters to whom he had given forty thousand francs of income ! I have seen wills burned; I have seen mothers robbing their children, husbands stealing from their wives, wives killing their husbands by making use of the love they inspired to drive them mad or witless, so that they might live in peace with a lover. I have seen women introducing their legitimate child to habits which will bring about its death, simply in order to benefit a love-child. I cannot relate all that I have seen, for I have witnessed crimes against which justice is powerless. In short, all the horrors which the novelists believe they have invented still fall short of the truth.»

Colonel Chabert

When he was fifty-one, Bernard-François married nineteen year-old Laure Sallambier, who came from a family of rich drapers in Paris. As her portrait shows, she was remarkably beautiful, intelligent and cultured, but she had a difficult character. As a child, Balzac felt deprived of affection, and he held this against his mother for many years. «What inner vanity could I, a new-born baby, possibly destroy ? What physical or moral defect in me could occasion my mother's coldness ? Was I the child of convenience, whose birth is merely fortuitous, or whose life is a lasting reproach ?» (*The Lily of the Valley*). Their relationship became embittered in later years by constant financial quarrels, which culminated in Madame Balzac's stormy visit to the rue Basse in 1841. «Madame de Berny was mother to me, and I grieved bitterly when God saw fit to take her from me, for if you only knew what my real mother is like !... She is both monster and monstrosity !» wrote Balzac to Madame Hanska in 1842. She nevertheless exerted an undoubted intellectual influence on her son. She was fascinated by esoteric doctrines, and had all the works of Boehm, Saint-Martin and Swedenborg, which the author of *Louis Lambert* and *Seraphîta* read with interest. Towards the end of her life, she also proved to be of great assistance to Balzac, meticulously carrying out the instructions he sent from Wierzschownia in preparation for the move to the rue Fortunée. Honoré was very close to his eldest sister, Laure, and dedicated *A Start in Life* to her. In 1820, she married an engineer from the Ponts et Chaussées, Eugène Surville. In 1858, she published a work devoted to her brother, entitled *Balzac, his life and work, based on his correspondence*.

At boarding school, Laure had a friend called Zulma Carraud, who met Balzac in 1919. She was married to Commander Carraud, an instructor at the Saint-Cyr military academy, and later director of the Angoulême powder factory

Portrait of
Laure Sallambier
Anon.
late xviiith century
pastel
inv. 96

Portrait of
Laure Balzac
as a child
Anon.
circa 1810
pastel
inv. 97

Portrait of
Laure de Berny
Anon.
circa 1815
miniature
inv. 516

«to say Laure without
saying I love you seems
to me a heresy of love
itself.»
To Madame de Berny,
April (?) 1822

from 1831 to 1834. Balzac often stayed with the Carrauds in Angoulême and in their property at Frapesle, near Issoudun. Zulma provided Balzac with information on Angoulême and Issoudun, where the action of *Lost Illusions* and *La Rabouilleuse* takes place, and also on provincial life in general. She was herself an austere Republican, and warned the writer against the temptations of Parisian life and aristocracy : «Leave the defence of people to the courtisans, and do not sully your well-earned reputation with solidarity of this kind. [...] Dear, dear friend, preserve your self-respect, even if the riches of English horses and Gothic chairs pass you by.» (3rd May 1832). First and foremost, however, she was an attentive and critical reader, and Balzac showed his appreciation by sending her small gifts, such as this inlaid casket, or copies of his own works, now preserved in the Maison de Balzac, each sent with his affectionate compliments. He also dedicated *The House of Nucingen* to her, in the following terms : «How can I not dedicate this work to you, Madame, whose intelligence and perspicacity are valuable treasures to your friends, and who are at once an entire public and the most indulgent of sisters ?»

But the woman who counted most in Balzac's youth, who remained an «indelible memory» as he says in a letter to Madame Hanska in 1837, was Laure de Berny, whom Balzac met in 1822 in Villeparisis. She was his «Dilecta», his loved one, «today and forever». An ebony casket and red leather blotting pad bearing the initials of her maiden name, L.H., recall that she was the daughter of one of the King's musicians, Joseph Hinner. She married a councillor of the Court, Gabriel de Berny, and was forty-five years old and the mother of nine children when she first met Balzac. Yet, as Balzac wrote to Madame Hanska, «Madame de B(erny), although married, was like a god to me, she was mother, companion, family, friend and advisor ; she created the writer, consoled the young man, nurtured taste, cried like a sister, laughed, and came every day like blessed sleep to quell the pain.»

DONNÉ
à Mᵐᵉ ZULMA CARRAUD
PAR
HONORÉ BALZAC
AUTEUR
DE LA COMÉDIE HUMAINE

Inlaid casket given
to Zulma Carraud
by Balzac
inv. 56

Balzac in society

Balzac was launched into salon society by the Duchess of Abrantès, whom he had met in 1825, who introduced him in turn to Madame Récamier, Madame Hamelin and Princess Bagration. He was also a frequent guest at Countess Merlin's salon, the studio of the painter Gérard and Nodier's receptions at the Arsenal, and became the friend of many artists and writers. In the years which followed his first successes, *Physiology of marriage* (1829) and *The Magic Skin* (1831), Balzac commissioned extravagant outfits from his tailor Buisson, who accepted a mention in *The Human Comedy* as payment, bought a tilbury in 1831, only to have it seized by the bailiffs, shared an «infernal box» at the Opera with the «lions», and frequented the most elegant cafés and fashionable salons, where his presence was much sought after : «His vivacity, eloquence and fluency were irresistible, and as everyone stopped talking in order to listen to him, the conversation soon lapsed into soliloquy, to his own and everyone's satisfaction. The original topic was soon forgotten and he jumped from anecdote to philosophical reflection, from moral observation to geographical description ; [...] he seemed somehow inspired from within, and conveyed with swift descriptive strokes the weird fantasmagorical images conceived in the black cells of his brain, using incomparable comic intensity and bouffe talent.» (Théophile Gautier, *L'Artiste*, 1858).

«Artistic tea flavoured with great men» by Grandville 1845 drawing inv. 598

Honoré de Balzac's
cane
by Le Cointe
1834
gold and turquoise
inv. 186

In 1834, Balzac ordered his famous turquoise-studded cane from the jeweller Le Cointe. It is now in the museum. The dragon and turquoises were originally part of a necklace worn by Madame Hanska as a young woman ; the head was engraved with the coat of arms of Balzac d'Entragues. This cane was soon to become the target of many a cartoonist and even inspired a book, *Monsieur de Balzac's Cane*, written by Delphine de Girardin in 1836, in which the cane was granted magic powers : «And there you have it; this frightful cane, like Giges' ring or Robert the Devil's golden branch, made its owner invisible.

[...] M. de Balzac, like popular princes in disguise, who visit poor dwellings or the palaces of the rich to put them to the test, hides in order to observe ; he watches, watches people who believe they are alone, who begin to think as never before; he observes geniuses as they get up in the morning, sentiments in dressing-gowns, vanity in nightcaps, passion in slippers, fury in caps, despair in nightshirts, and then he puts the whole lot in a book ! ... and the book creates a furore in France, is translated in Germany and counterfeited in Belgium, and M. de Balzac is hailed as a genius ! Pure charlatanism ! It is the cane we should be admiring and not its owner ; his only merit lies in the way he uses it.»

Nevertheless in 1835 Balzac was writing to the marquess of Custine : «I was fast becoming an ordinary man by allowing society to take over» and on 16th May 1843 he wrote to Madame Hanska «The great achievements in my life are my works.»

Passy, 1st January 1844 ! ...

«I hardly need tell you that as soon as I awoke I seized the letter upon which my head had rested and that these are my very first lines. I am writing at 8 o'clock in the
morning, with the sun filtering through my window, wrea-
thing my desk, drapes and papers in a red scarf. Surely there are enough omens here. Are they to be trusted ? The
beauty of this early morning is difficult to conceive. The sky
is blue, with a few clouds accentuating its intensity, and the
heights of Issy and Meudon are bathed in light; I can see
them as I write. No! this must surely be God's way of fore-
casting happiness !»

Letters to Madame Hanska

Balzac's study
by Robert Doisneau
1986
photograph
inv. 89-91

On 2nd October 1841, a year after moving into the rue Basse, Balzac drew up an agreement with the publishers Furne, Hetzel, Paulin and Dubochet, granting them «exclusive rights to print and sell his complete works under the generic title *The Human Comedy*».

A number of documents preserved in the Maison de Balzac help to pinpoint landmarks in the construction of *The Human Comedy*. In a letter to Baron Gérard, dated 1831, Balzac announces that «the general system of his work is beginning to take shape». In 1834, Madame Charles Béchet, whose portrait hangs in the museum, begins publishing a «Study of XIXth century morals» in twelve volumes. The same year Balzac writes to Doctor Nacquart : «When everything is actually published, in three or four years time, you will be surprised to find that you were busy advocating a great work when it was already in your hands.» Finally, in a letter addressed to his publisher in 1840, the writer draws up a plan for the work and mentions the title for the first time : *The Human Comedy*.

This publication of *The Human Comedy*, usually referred to as the Furne edition, demanded a tremendous amount of proof-reading by the novelist «*The Human Comedy* takes up 200 hours per month, as I have to read each proof twice over, and I have also had to go through the copy which serves as manuscript. This makes 3 rereadings at 3 hours a page, and there are 30 per volume : just imagine what this represents, although I never mention the task to you. It is colossal, for I have to find my mistakes and then correct them. It is a perpetual test of literary conscientiousness.» (*Letters to Madame Hanska*, 7th December 1842).

In 1844, to avoid leaving "this monument in an inexplicable state", Balzac drew up an initial «catalogue of works for *The Hum[an] Comed[y]*, there are 125 all together, I have

Portrait
of Madame Béchet
by Eugène Goyet
oil on canvas
inv. 546

only 40 more to do, which should ensure that our life is gently occupied for the next ten years, very gently, for I am unwilling to waste a single minute of the youth, harmonious love and pleasure still allotted to us». (*Letters to Madame Hanska*, 26th July 1844).

He had the catalogue printed in 1845, but added twelve more, which now left 50 works «left to do». *The Human Comedy* was never to be completed, but tens of thousands of lines were written at this modest desk.

The study has been preserved as it was in Balzac's day, «hung with red velvet» and containing the original furniture, and it is easy to imagine the writer, in his monk's habit, «harnessed» to his small table which, as he wrote to Madame Hanska on 21st June 1834, «witnessed all my thoughts, anguish, suffering, despair, joys, everything !».

Apart from the table, armchair and bust by David d'Angers, a number of other personal objects have found their way into the study : the coffee pot bearing Balzac's initials recalls his excessive use of this «modern-day stimulant»; the vase in Bohemian crystal presented to Balzac by a Belgian lady admirer, Ida de Bocarmé, illustrates the cult following

Engraved
gold watch
belonging
to Balzac
1846
inv. 88-21

generated by the writer : «She had a glass brought over from Bohemia, a monumental object with *Divo Balzac* engraved upon it and two muses, one crowning me and the other inscribing on a folio : *Comédie humaine* ! It is in appalling taste, but to each his own, you know. The poor woman is called Bettina, is 45 but looks 50 and has teeth held together with gold, but she's a decent sort. She has painted the entire *Armorial of a Study of Morals*, featuring one hundred coats of arms, it is a work of art.» (*Letters to Madame Hanska*, 21st March 1844).

Another donation was made to the museum in 1988, an engraved gold watch with the Balzac d'Entragues coat of arms, made in Geneva by Liodet in 1846.

According to Balzac's letters, the walls of the study were covered in pictures, but these have not been tracked down, apart from one of Madame Hanska and another of Wierzschownia castle, which Balzac always had in front of him; they complete the décor of this room in which Balzac gave shape to *The Human Comedy*, whilst still keeping up his correspondence with «The Foreigner» : «Writing to you means returning to the paradise of my memories and the hell of postponed hopes [...] : you represent my undoing, my happy daydreams, my meandering soul ! Oh ! If only you could see my expression when I look from portrait to landscape, and realise how much life and eloquence is there. A thousand pages of letters are summed up in five seconds !» (*Letters to Madame Hanska*, 29th [April 1842].)

«The property is just like another Louvre
and covers as much land as an entire
county.»
To Laure Surville, 8th October 1847.

View of
Wierzschownia
castle
by N. Orda
circa 1860
lithograph
inv. 417

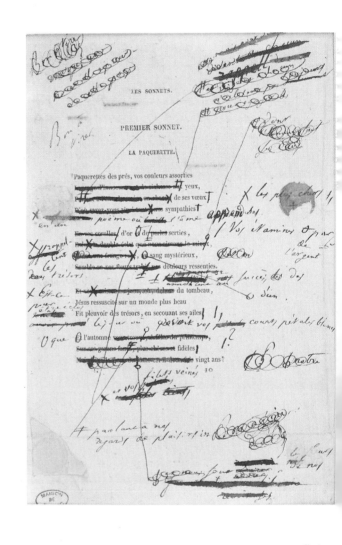

*Illusions
perdues
by Honoré
de Balzac
Corrected
proof
inv. 89-21*

Portrait of
Madame Hanska
by Sowgen
circa 1825
miniature on ivory
inv. 34

Eveline Hanska was born in the province of Kiew into a noble Polish family, the Rzewuskis, in 1805 or 1806. A miniature on ivory, by Sowgen, depicts the graceful traits of the young girl at the time of her marriage to Count Hanski, who owned vast domains in the Ukraine and was twenty-two years her senior. Eveline spoke several languages fluently, including French, and to break up the tedium and loneliness of her life in Wierzschownia, spent much of her time reading books from France. It was in this way that she discovered Balzac.

Between 1832 and 1848, Balzac kept up a voluminous correspondence with «The Foreigner», a romantic novel and «diary» in one.

Balzac first met Madame Hanska in Neuchâtel, on 25th September 1833. He saw her again the following year, in Geneva, and again in 1835 in Vienna, but there followed a gap of eight years before they met again in St. Petersburg. When Count Hanski died in 1841, Balzac hoped to marry Madame Hanska at long last, but she postponed any wedding plans. They travelled together in 1845, and Balzac joined her in the Ukraine in September 1847. Apart from a brief trip to Paris in 1848, Balzac spent the last two years of his life in Wierzschownia. On 14th March 1850, Madame Hanska married Balzac in Berdichev. Five months later, on 18th August, Balzac died at his home in the rue Fortunée.

The house in the
rue Fortunée
by Dargaud
1880
oil on wood
inv. 965

Anxious to keep Madame Hanska in the style to which she was accustomed, Balzac purchased, on 28th September 1846, a part of the «folly» belonging to the financier Beaujon, situated in the rue Fortunée (now called rue Balzac). His last home is portrayed in a small picture by Dargaud and in photographs by Cary : the long, narrow façade «reminiscent of army barracks», the two sitting-rooms, and the «surprise» Balzac had in store for Madame Hanska, a tribune which led directly from the apartments into the chapel of St. Nicholas. Balzac undertook considerable renovation work and devised the interior decoration down to the minutest detail, indulging his «bric-à-bracomania». He had been collecting works of art since 1844, storing them in the rue Basse. An example of this is the Christ, attributed by the novelist to Bouchardon, in a frame attributed to the sculptor Brustolone, which was «estimated at 3000 F, but which Mme de B(rugnol) picked up by chance for 150 F !»

Victor Hugo, who came to visit Balzac during his final illness, was flabbergasted by the opulence of the house, particularly the staircase, and described it in Choses vues. One of Balzac's bookcases and the magnificent inlaid door of the first-floor sitting-room are eloquent reminders of the splendours of the rue Fortunée.

Following Balzac's death, Madame Hanska became the companion of the painter Jean Gigoux, who drew a number of portraits of Eve, her daughter Anna and son-in-law Georges Mniszech.

Madame Hanska lived in the rue Fortunée right up to her death in 1882, at which time the entire Balzac collections were dispersed by auction at the Salle Drouot. The major part of the manuscripts and correspondence were then acquired by an erudite Belgian collector, Viscount Spoelberch de Lovenjoul, who donated them to the Institut de France.

The Maison de Balzac itself continues to acquire pictures, objects, books and signed documents from collectors and public auction. In 1989, a number of original editions of Balzac's works were purchased, originating from his personal library, as well as the original edition of *Prophètes du passé* by Barbey d'Aurevilly, bound with the coat of arms of Tsar Nicholas 1st, which was presented to Madame Hanska two years after the writer's death with the following superb dedication :

«To Madame H. de Balzac
As a sign of deep respect
This book was destined for His Majesty the Emperor of Russia
But I would rather place it in the hands of the wife of a man of genius, — someone who was for all we xixth century writers, a literary Sovereign, — Our Emperor !»

Portrait of Anna Hanska by Jean Gigoux pastel inv. 871

«Anna possesses something even more precious than beauty, it is grace, a noble grace.
The angelic purity of her soul lends a certain divinity to her traits, her movements and her expressions, and the artist cannot but be captivated.»

A large number of prints from newspapers and albums, illustrated editions and translations in all languages testify to the far-reaching impact of Balzac's work worldwide, from the xixth century to the present day. All these collections are displayed in rotation on the lower floor of the museum.

The most significant prints include the collective portraits in which Balzac appears surrounded by contemporary celebrities, such as Grandville's «Grande Course au clocher académique» or Benjamin Roubaud's «Grand Chemin de la Posterité». In 1854, Balzac was portrayed in Nadar's Pantheon beside George Sand (ref.n° 2).

Successive illustrated editions also underline the artistic repercussions of Balzac's work. During his lifetime, Balzac frequented the most famous artists of the day, the brothers Johannot, Grandville, Gavarni, who owed his introduction to the journal «L'Artiste» to Balzac, Henry Monnier who created the figure of Monsieur Prudhomme. In 1841, shortly after signing the publication agreement for *The Human Comedy*, Balzac provided the publisher Hetzel with the themes for the illustrations contained in each volume and their respective artists «I will provide further directions for the 3rd and 4th volumes of *Scenes of private life* as they occur to me, but it is imperative that the artists read the book.» (Passy, October 1841). Most of these projects came to nothing. Balzac was unable to persuade Ingres, for instance, to «do» *Eugénie Grandet*. Great names did appear on the Furne editions, however : Meissonnier, Tony Johannot, Bertall, Nanteuil, Monnier...

As regards the xxth century, the Maison de Balzac has managed to acquire the bronze and terracotta statuettes carved by P. Ripert in the Twenties and Charles Huard's notebooks and sketches for the illustration of Balzac's complete works published in 40 volumes by Conard, between 1912 and

*Traité des excitants
modernes*
by Honoré de Balzac
with illustrations
by Pierre Alechinsky
1989
linos
inv. 91-1

1940. A donation by Madame Pierre de Belay was also made to the museum, representing her husband's entire collection of drawings for three great novels, *A Dark Affair*, *Cousin Bette* and *César Birotteau*. The variety of techniques — pencil, pen, gouache, sanguine — often applied simultaneously, demonstrates the artist's constant creative experimentation.

The museum reserves have been enriched still further over the last few years with illustrated works, drawings and engravings executed by Quint, Jouve, Jeanniot, Léonor Fini... In 1989, Pierre Alechinsky illustrated Honoré de Balzac's *Treaty of modern-day stimulants*. The museum has retained a copy of the original edition, which includes seven etchings and fourteen linoengravings as well as the linos carved by Alechinsky himself. By acquiring contemporary creations such as these, the museum is able to demonstrate the lasting impact of Balzac's work and show the new forms of illustration it inspires today.

«Slowly coaxing out with a knife and gouge the drawings created in swift brushstrokes, certain incomparable descriptions, comments and turns of phrase are necessarily overlooked» writes Alechinsky, adding «Illustration does not imply competition.»

Finally a vast collection of works and archive material enables one to retrace the origins of Balzac's statue and evoke his cult following at the end of the xixth century. The most notable objects here are the documents concerning the subscription launched in 1883 by the Société des gens de lettres, of which Balzac was founder and president, an unfinished model by the sculptor Chapu, who died in 1891, and various projects planned by Marquet de Vasselot, who exhibited in 1896 a symbolist portrait of Balzac as a winged sphinx, now familiar in photographic form, and also created a bas-relief in 1888, representing over one hundred characters from *The Human Comedy*. This work, which was cast in bronze in 1982, is now displayed in the museum garden. It was Falguière's project which was finally chosen, and the statue was inaugurated in 1902, on the corner of the rue Balzac and the avenue de Friedland. Rodin's celebrated statue features in a rare poster from Prague, where an exhibition of the sculptor's work was held in 1902, and in a remarkable original plaster study of the head.

Study
for Rodin's
statue of Balzac
circa 1897
plaster
inv. 89-97

The library is situated in the former stables, on the ground-floor overlooking the rue Berton. It is a research and study centre devoted to Balzac and the Romantics and is open to all. It includes :

- the original reserves of first editions, completed by almost every subsequent edition of Balzac's work, both rare and commonplace, including foreign translations. The books printed by Balzac himself at the beginning of his career are also featured, together with a growing collection of xixth century newspapers, bindings and illustrations from the Romantic period,

- the documentation and research reserves, which include a considerable number of general reference works and studies devoted not only to Balzac but to the Romantic era in general : works by Balzac's celebrated peers, theses, conferences, exhibition catalogues, articles and special issues, French and foreign periodicals from the past and present day, documentary files...,

- the specific reserves : manuscripts, prints, photographs and microfilms (available by appointment).

«In Paris there are certain streets which have fallen into as much disrepute as a man branded with infamy ; there are also noble streets, straightforwardly decent streets and young streets upon whose morality the public has not yet formed an opinion ; there are murderous streets, streets more ancient than the most aged dowagers, respectable streets, streets which are always clean, streets which are always dirty, working-class, industrious, mercantile streets. In short, the streets of Paris have human qualities, and their physiognomy imprints certain ideas in us against which we are totally defenceless. There are streets of questionable reputation in which you would not like to live, and others in which you would willingly reside. Some, like the rue Montmartre, start off in superb style and tail off further down. The rue de la Paix is a wide street, a major street ; but it inspires none of those graciously noble reflections which spring to the impressionable mind in the middle of the rue Royale, and certainly lacks the majesty of the place Vendôme. If you wander along the streets of the île Saint-Louis, you do not need to look further than the solitude and dreary appearance of the houses and deserted mansions to explain the uneasy melancholy which pervades your being. This island, the cemetery of the farmers-general, is like Paris' Venice. The Bourse is all prattle, bustle and harlotry, and is only beautiful by moonlight, at two o'clock in the morning ; during the day it is a condensation of Paris ; at night it is like some Grecian dream. Is not the rue Traversière-Saint-Honoré an infamous street ? There are mean little houses with two casement windows, where vice, crime and poverty are present on every floor. The narrow streets facing North, which only enjoy a ray of sunlight three or four times a year, are sinister streets where murder is committed with impunity ; today Justice closes its eyes to them, although in the olden days Parliament might have summoned the police lieutenant to account, or would at least have delivered some kind of judgment against the street, as it did against the bewigged canons of Beauvais. Yet Monsieur Benoiston du Châteauneuf has proved that the mortality in these streets is twice as high as the average. To sum up these ideas, take a single example, that of the rue Fromenteau, known not only for murder but for prostitution. These observations, which would be incomprehensible outside Paris, will doubtless be seized upon by those men of learning and reflection, of poetry and pleasure, who, wandering within the city walls, feast on the delectable enjoyments it offers from morn till night ; by those who find Paris the most delightful of monsters : a pretty woman at times, at others a miserable old hag ; as freshly minted as a new coin here, as elegant as a lady of fashion there. A monster from head to toe, in fact ! its head is the garret, full of science and genius ; the top floors are replete stomachs ; the feet are the shops, treading the hustle and bustle of trade. And what an active life the monster leads. No sooner has the rattle of the last carriages died down than he is stretching his extremities at the city gates. The doors yawn open and turn on their hinges like a huge lobster, invisibly operated by thirty thousand men or women, who each live in six square feet, with a kitchen, a workshop, a bed, children, a garden, unable to see clearly yet needing to see everything. Imperceptibly the joints begin to crack, movement spreads, the street starts talking. By midday, everything is alive, the chimneys are smoking, the monster eats ; then it roars and stirs a thousand legs. What a sight ! But Paris, he who has not admired your sombre landscapes, shot here and there with glimpses of light and your deep, silent alleyways ; he who has not listened to your murmurs between midnight and two o'clock, still knows nothing of your true poetry, of your strange and striking contrasts. A handful of devotees, who never walk in heedless inattention, do know how to savour their Paris, so familiar with its aspect that they notice the slightest wart, spot or blemish. For the others, Paris is still the same monstrous miracle, an extraordinary assembly of movement, machines and thoughts, the city of a thousand novels, the brains behind the world.»

Ferragus

2 - BALZAC'S PARISIAN HOMES

Rue de Lesdiguières

«I lived at that time in a little street with which you are probably unfamiliar, the rue de Lesdiguières : it starts at the rue Saint-Antoine, opposite a fountain near the place de la Bastille, and opens out into the rue de la Cerisaie. Love of science had lodged me in a garret, where I worked by night, and I spent the day in a nearby library belonging to MONSIEUR. I lived frugally and had accepted all the monastic conditions such a working life demands. When the weather was fine, I very occasionally allowed myself a walk along the boulevard Bourdon. Only one passion led me away from my studious habits; but was it not in itself a form of study ? I went to observe the life and customs of the street and the characters of its inhabitants. As poorly dressed as the workmen themselves and indifferent to the proprieties, they had no reason to be on their guard ; I was able to mingle with them, watch them concluding their bargains and quarelling as they left work. In me, observation was already intuitive, it penetrated the soul without neglecting the body ; or more precisely, seized the external details so swiftly that it immediately transcended them ; it allowed me to live the life of the individual upon whom it was directed, letting me substitute myself for him as the dervish in *The Arabian Nights* assumed the body and soul of the people to whom he uttered his spell.

When, between eleven o'clock and midnight, I came across a workman and his wife returning from the Ambigu-Comique, I found distraction in following them from the boulevard du Pont-aux-Choux to the boulevard Beaumarchais. These decent people first talked of the play they had seen; little by little they came to talk of their own affairs; the mother dragged her child along, heeding neither its whines nor its requests; the couple worked out how much money they would receive the next day and spent it in twenty different ways. Then there would be household details, complaints over the excessive cost of potatoes or the endless winter and price of fuel, lively discussions on the amount owed to the baker; finally the arguments became bitter and each of them revealed his character in picturesque words. When I heard these people. I took on their life, I could feel their rags on my back, I walked in their worn shoes ; their wishes and needs passed from their soul to mine or from mine to theirs. This was a daydream. I became as indignant as they over the tyranny of the workshop foremen, or the immoral practice of making them return without pay. To break with habit, stepping outside myself by giving free rein to my moral faculties, such was my distraction. To what do I owe this gift ? Is it second sight ? Is it one of those habits which leads to madness if abused ? I have never tried to determine its cause ; I have it and make use of it, that's all.»

Facino Cane

Rue des Batailles

«The half of the boudoir in which Henri now found himself described a softly graceful curve, contrasting with the other half, which was perfectly rectangular and resplendent with a gold and white marble fireplace. He had entered by a side door concealed by a sumptuous tapestry curtain, with a window opposite. The horseshoe was adorned with a genuine Turkish divan, in other words a mattress placed upon the floor, but as wide as a bed, fifty feet in circumference, in white cashmere offset by black and poppy-red silk rosettes in a lozenge pattern. The back of this huge bed rose several inches higher than its many cushions, tastefully matched to give even greater opulence. The boudoir was hung with red fabric overlaid with folds of hollowed and billowing Indian muslin like a Corinthian column, trimmed at the top and bottom with a poppy-red band with black arabesque designs. Beneath the muslin the poppy-red became pink, the colour of love, echoed in the curtains which were in Indian muslin lined with pink taffeta and bordered with poppy-red and black fringes. Six silver-gilt sconces, each of them bearing two candles, were attached to the drapes at equal distances to light the divan. The ceiling, from the centre of which hung a chandelier of dull silver-gilt, was dazzlingly white, with a gilded cornice. The rug ressembled an Oriental shawl, recalling the designs and evoking the poetry of Persia, where the hands of slaves had worked it. The furniture was upholstered in white cashmere, set off by black and poppy-red trimmings. The clock and candelabra, everything was in gold and white marble. The only table was covered with a cashmere tablecloth.

Elegant flower-stands contained every kind of rose, and either white or red flowers. Every detail seemed to have been thought out with minutely loving care. Richness had never been so cunningly disguised as elegance, expressing grace and inspiring voluptuousness. Everything was designed to warm the blood of the coldest mortal. The sheen of the drapes, whose colour altered with every viewing angle, white and pink in turn, harmonised with the lighting effects infused into the diaphanous folds of the muslin, producing an impression of clouds. The soul is curiously attracted to white, love is happiest in red, and gold flatters the passions because it holds the power to fulfil their fantasies. Thus everything vague and mysterious in man, all his inexplicable affinities, found an involuntary echo here. In this perfect harmony was a concert of colour to which the soul responded with voluptuous, tentative and fluctuating ideas.»

The Girl with the Golden Eyes

Les Jardies at Ville d'Avray

«I purchased two years ago, above the ponds of Ville d'Avray, on the road to Versailles, some twenty acres of meadows, a strip of woodland and a fine little fruit garden. At the end of the meadows, the ground has been excavated in such a way as to obtain a pond about three acres wide, in the middle of which a prettily contrived island has been left. The two pretty wooded hills which enclose this little valley distil ravishing little streams which flow through my grounds, where they have been astutely channelled by my landscape gardener. These streams run into the ponds of the crown, glimpsed in the distance. This admirably designed little park is, according to the nature of the terrain, surrounded by hedges, walls and deep ditches, so that no panorama is lost. Half-way up the hill, flanked by the woods of la Ronce, delightfully situated before a meadow sloping down to the pond, a chalet has been built for me, the outside of which resembles in every particular the one travellers admire on the road from Sion to Brigg, with which I was so taken on my return from Italy. Inside, its elegance bears comparison with the most illustrious chalets. A stone's throw from this rustic dwelling is a charming house which communicates with the chalet by an underground passage and contains the kitchen, servants' quarters, stables and outhouses. Before all these constructions in brick, the eye only sees a gracefully simple façade surrounded by shrubbery. The gardeners' lodge forms another structure and conceals the entrance to the orchards and vegetable gardens.»

Memoirs of Two Young Wives

1799	Balzac born in Tours (20th May).
1807-1813	Attends school at the collège de Vendôme.
1814	Family moves to Paris.
1816	Enrols in the Law Faculty.
	Articled to Maître Guillonet-Merville and Maître Passez.
1819	Moves to the rue Lesdiguières.
1821-1825	Publishes several novels under pseudonyms.
1822	Meets Laure de Berny.
1826-1828	Launches the "H.Balzac" printing works, rue Visconti
1829	Death of Balzac's father.
	Publication of *The Chouans*, first novel written under Balzac's own name.
1830	Intense literary and salon activity.
1832	First of Madame Hanska's letters to Balzac.
1833	Balzac meets Madame Hanska at Neuchâtel.
1834	*Old Goriot* (plans drawn up for a sequel)
1836	Death of Madame de Berny.
1837	Moves to Les Jardies.
1840	Moves to Passy, rue Basse (now rue Raynouard).
1841	Publication agreement signed for *The Human Comedy* (Furne editions). Death of Count Hanski.
1842	Writes foreword of *The Human Comedy*. First delivery of *The Human Comedy*.
1843	Travels to St.Petersburg.
1845	Plans the «catalogue of works for *The Human Comedy*». Visits Germany, France, the Netherlands and Italy with Madame Hanska.
1846	Buys house in the rue Fortunée (now rue Balzac).
1848-1850	Stays in Wierzschownia. Marries Madame Hanska (14th March). Death of Balzac rue Fortunée (18th August).

Visitors' entrance
47, rue Raynouard, 75016 Paris

Hours of opening
Museum : Tuesday to Sunday
10.00 to 17.40
Closed on Mondays and public holidays
Library : Tuesday to Saturday
10.00 to 17.40
Closed on Sundays, Mondays and public
holidays

Transport
Metro Passy / La Muette
RER C Boulainvilliers and Radio France
Bus n° 32

Communication and activity centre
- Groups :
Lecture tours on request
- Individual visitors :
Guided tours on Tuesdays at 14.30
(dates available from museum)
- Activities for schools
- Information : tél. 42 24 56 38

Publications available
Dessins d'écrivains français au XIXe siècle,
1983 - *Balzac et le Monde des Coquins,*
1985 - *Les Ecrivains vus par Robert
Doisneau,* 1986 - *De la maison au
musée,* 1987 - *Benjamin Roubaud et le
Panthéon Charivarique,* 1988 - *Balzac et
la Révolution française,* 1988 - *Dantan
Jeune : caricatures et portraits de la
société romantique,* 1989 - *Alechinsky à
la Maison de Balzac. Traité des excitants
modernes,* 1989 - *Nadar : caricatures et
photographies,* 1990

Curators' department
47, rue Raynouard
75016 Paris
Tél. : 42 24 56 38

Authors : Judith Meyer-Petit, Anne Panchout

Photoengraving : Bussière Arts graphiques, Paris

Flashing : Delta +, Levallois-Perret

Printing : Imprimerie Alençonnaise, Paris

Data base operator : Berthe Bogerbe

Graphic design :
Gilles Beaujard, assisted by Viviane Linois

Production : Florence Jakubowicz

English translation : Caroline Taylor-Bouché

First printed by imprimerie Alençonnaise in Alençon, July 1991

Individual orders (France) :
Minitel 3615 CAPITALE

Cover : Photo Daniel Lifermann

© Paris-Musées, 1991
Registration of copyright 3rd quarter 1991
ISBN 2-87900-050-5

Photographic acknowledgments :
Photothèque des musées de la Ville de Paris,
© by SPADEM 1991
Gérard Weiss p.6
Robert Doisneau p.28
Galerie Lelong p.37